Siamese

and Other Short-haired Cats

Editor in Chief: Paul A. Kobasa
Supplementary Publications: Lisa Kwon, Christine Sullivan, Scott Thomas
Research: Mike Barr, Timothy J. Breslin, Cheryl Graham, Barbara Lightner, Loranne Shields
Graphics and Design: Kathy Creech, Sandra Dyrlund, Charlene Epple, Tom Evans
Permissions: Janet Peterson
Indexing: David Pofelski
Prepress and Manufacturing: Anne Dillon, Carma Fazio, Anne Fritzinger, Steven Hueppchen, Tina Ramirez
Writer: Karen Ingebretsen

For information about other World Book publications, visit our Web site at http://www.worldbook.com or call 1-800-WORLDBK (967-5325).

For information about sales to schools and libraries, call 1-800-975-3250 (United States); 1-800-837-5365 (Canada).

World Book, Inc.
233 N. Michigan Avenue
Chicago, IL 60601
U.S.A.

Library of Congress Cataloging-in-Publication Data

Siamese and other short-haired cats.
　　p. cm. -- (World Book's animals of the world)
　　Summary: "An introduction to Siamese and other short-haired cats, presented in a highly illustrated, question and answer format. Features include fun facts, glossary, resource list, index, and scientific classification list"--Provided by publisher.
　　Includes bibliographical references and index.
　　ISBN-13: 978-0-7166-1335-0
　　ISBN-10: 0-7166-1335-2
　　1. Siamese cat--Miscellanea--Juvenile literature. 2. Cats—Miscellanea--Juvenile literature. I. World Book, Inc. II. Series.
SF4449.S5S53 2007
636.8'25--dc22
　　　　　　　　　　2006017463

Printed in Malaysia
1 2 3 4 5 6 7 8 09 08 07 06

Picture Acknowledgments: Cover: © Yann Arthus-Bertrand, Corbis; © Chanan; © Rolf Kopfle, Ardea London; © Jean Michel Labat, Ardea London; © Jerry Shulman, SuperStock.

© Dynamic Graphics Group/Creatas/Alamy Images 27; © FLPA/Alamy Images 23; © Yann Arthus-Bertrand, Corbis 35, 43; © Chanan 31, 39; © Corbis 51; © Corbis/Bettmann 11; © John Daniels, Ardea London 53, 55; © Vassil Donev, EPA/Landov 59; © Dorling Kindersley 4, 47; © Margie Hayes, Alamy Images 61; © Marc Henrie, Dorling Kindersley 41; © Mitsuaki Iwago, Minden Pictures 5, 37, 45; © Dave King, Dorling Kindersley 3, 7; © Rolf Kopfle, Ardea London 17, 29; © Jean Michel Labat, Ardea London 49; © Carolyn A. McKeone 19, 25; © Steven Puetzer, Nonstock/Jupiter Images 21; © Keith Ringland, Oxford Scientific/Jupiter Images 57; © Manfred Rutz, Getty Images 5, 33; © Peter H. Sprosty, Photonica/Getty Images 15.

Illustrations: WORLD BOOK illustrations by John Fleck 9; WORLD BOOK illustration by Paul Perreault 13.

Siamese

and Other Short-haired Cats

World Book, Inc.
a Scott Fetzer company
Chicago

Contents

What Is a Short-haired Cat? 6

What Is Under All That Fur? 8

How Did the Siamese Breed Develop? 10

What Color Does That Siamese Come In? 12

What Kind of Personality Might a Siamese Have? 14

What Should You Look for When Choosing a Siamese Kitten? 16

Should You Get an Older Siamese Instead of a Kitten? 18

What Does a Siamese Eat? 20

Where Should a Siamese Sleep? 22

How Do You Groom a Siamese? 24

Can You Train Your Siamese? 26

What Kinds of Exercise or Play Are Needed? 28

How Can You Help a Siamese Care for Its Young? 30

Does a Siamese Cat Have a Point? 32

What Is a Purebred, Crossbred, or Pedigreed Cat? 34

What Is an Aby Cat? 36

What Is a Colorpoint Shorthair?...........................38

What Short-haired Cat Might Bring Luck? 40

What Are Some Other Breeds of Short-haired Cats? 42

How Keen Are a Cat's Senses?...........................44

How Do Cats Communicate? 46

Why Does a Cat Twine Itself Around Your Ankles? 48

How Can You Make Your Home Safe for a Cat?...............50

What Basic Equipment Is Needed for a Cat?................52

What Is a Cat Show Like? 54

What Are Some Common Signs of Illness in Cats? 56

What Routine Veterinary Care Is Needed? 58

What Are Your Responsibilities as an Owner?...............60

Short-haired Cat Fun Facts...........................62

Glossary...........................63

Index and Resource List 64

Cat Classification 65

What Is a
Short-haired Cat?

All cats are members of the family Felidae
(FEE luh dy). This family includes the lion, tiger,
panther, and leopard. It also includes domestic cats.
Domestic cats are smaller members of the cat
family that were tamed by humans long ago and
which are now often kept as pets. Whether small
or large, all cats are carnivores, or meat-eaters,
and they are skillful hunters. In addition, all cats are
warm-blooded and are mammals, animals that feed
their young with milk made by the mother.

Short-haired cats are domestic cats that have
short instead of long fur. A short-haired cat may
have a single or double coat. A single coat is usually
made up of fine or silky fur that clings close to the
body. Siamese cats and Burmese cats have single
coats. A double coat is made up of long hairs called
guard hairs and a thick, downy undercoat. Manx and
Russian blue cats (see page 42) have double coats.

A Siamese cat

What Is Under
All That Fur?

Under their fur, cats have long, powerful bodies. The skeleton of a cat is similar in structure to other meat-eating mammals. Cats, however, have short, strong jaws and sharp teeth that are especially well suited for hunting. Their tail is an extension of their backbone. A cat uses its tail to keep its balance.

Most cats have five toes on each front paw. The innermost toe is like a thumb that is helpful for catching prey. Each toe ends in a sharp, hooklike claw. The claws are usually retracted (held back) under the skin. But, when the claws are needed, they can be quickly extended. Several spongy pads of thick skin cover the bottoms of a cat's feet. These pads cushion the paws and allow a cat to move quietly.

A Siamese cat is like most other cats, but its body is often longer and more slender, and it has a thinner tail. A Siamese usually has a wedge-shaped head with large, pointed ears.

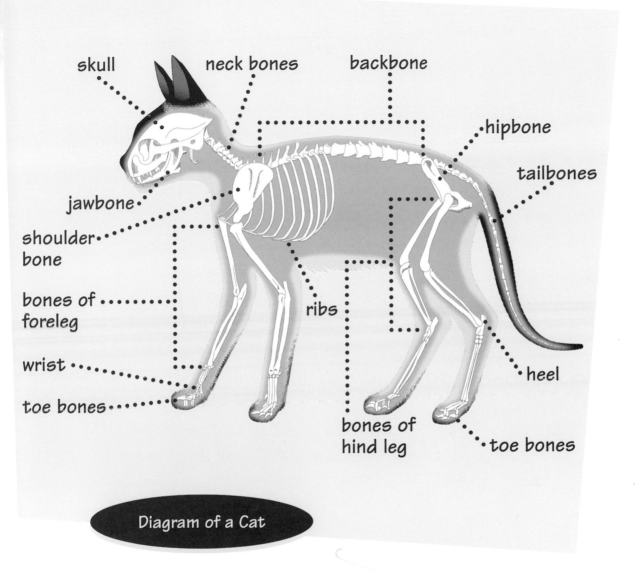

skull

neck bones

backbone

hipbone

tailbones

jawbone

shoulder
bone

bones of
foreleg

ribs

wrist

toe bones

bones of
hind leg

heel

toe bones

Diagram of a Cat

9

How Did the Siamese Breed Develop?

A breed is a group of animals that has the same type of ancestors. People develop different breeds of cats by selectively mating animals with desirable traits (features or characteristics).

The Siamese breed originated in Thailand (formerly called Siam). In 1884, a pair of Siamese cats was brought to the United Kingdom. Their offspring won many prizes at cat shows, and the breed soon gained worldwide popularity. Siamese were first introduced into the United States in 1890.

Of the 24 short-haired breeds recognized by the Cat Fanciers' Association (CFA), the major cat association in the United States, the Siamese is the most popular.

Prize-winning Siamese from the 1930's with their owner

What Color Does That Siamese Come In?

Siamese cats are known for their colorpoint coats. A colorpoint coat is a solid color over the trunk of the body and a contrasting color on the points—that is, the face, ears, feet, and tail (see page 32). Siamese cats can have a number of colorings, but the four major colors of the breed are:

- chocolate—A cat with ivory fur and milk-chocolate colored points.

- lilac—A cat with white fur with a pale blue coloring (blue really means gray, but breeders often refer to gray as "blue") and pinkish-gray points.

- blue—A cat with bluish-white fur and dark gray points.

- seal—A cat with cream-colored fur and dark brown points. This last coloring is the most common.

Chocolate

Lilac

Blue

Seal

The four major colorings of Siamese

13

What Kind of Personality Might a Siamese Have?

Siamese cats are very "talkative." Most Siamese are louder than cats of other breeds, and their "speech" varies more in tone and pitch than other breeds. Siamese can be very insistent, too; they often issue loud, mournful meows until they get your attention.

Siamese are very affectionate. Most are active and playful, but they can also be moody and impatient. They do not do well when left alone for long periods; many Siamese need the company of another cat or dog for those times when their owner cannot devote attention to them.

Siamese cats also are curious about everything around them, and they can be mischief-makers.

A playful Siamese
hides under a rug

What Should You Look for When Choosing a Siamese Kitten?

The most important thing about choosing a pet kitten is that it is healthy. Some signs of good health are: alertness; normal body weight; bright, clear eyes; a clean, slightly moist nose; clean teeth and pink gums; quiet breathing (no wheezing, coughing, or sneezing); no lumps or bumps on the body; clean ears with no unpleasant smell; and a glossy coat that feels clean to the touch.

Try to choose a cat that is not at either personality extreme. Neither choose a cat that is very shy and fearful, nor one that is wild and frenzied.

A Siamese kitten
exploring

17

Should You Get
an Older Siamese
Instead of a Kitten?

There are a number of advantages to adopting an older Siamese. Often, older cats have already been spayed or neutered so that they are unable to produce young. An older cat may also have been tested for infectious diseases and is often already used to living with people.

Animal shelters in your area may well have Siamese cats available for adoption. There are also a number of sites on the Internet devoted to the rescue of purebred cats, including Siamese. These sites feature abandoned cats for adoption to loving homes. Or, breeders may sometimes have cats that are being retired from the show ring that are available to be adopted.

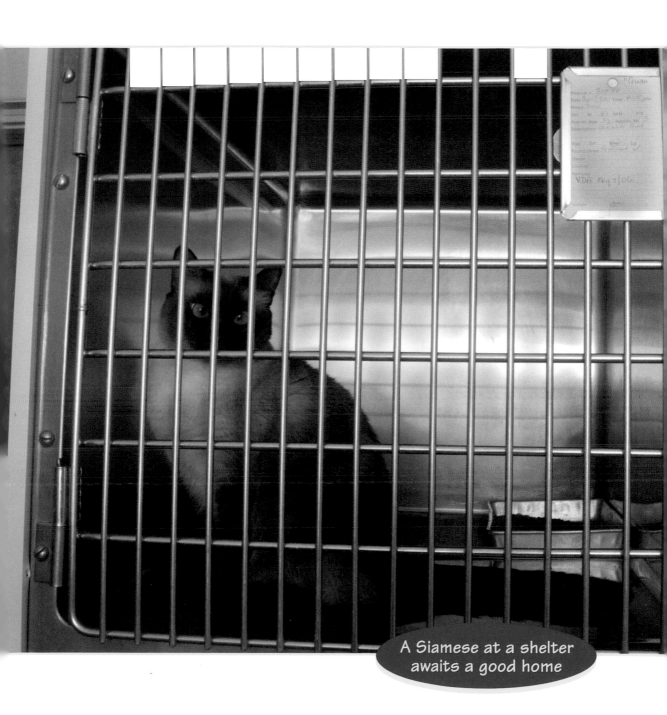

A Siamese at a shelter
awaits a good home

What Does a Siamese Eat?

Most Siamese eat a diet of commercial canned or dry cat food. Whatever type of food you choose, you should vary the flavors given. Otherwise, a cat may become so used to eating only one flavor that it refuses everything else.

Some people feed their Siamese cats limited types of table food (human food), such as cottage cheese, egg yolks, and scraps of meat and vegetables. If you choose to do this, you should feed your cat table food only in very small quantities in addition to cat food. Table food does not provide a cat with a balanced, nutritious diet, which packaged food does.

Like all cats, Siamese should have fresh drinking water at all times.

A Siamese asks
for dinner

Where Should a Siamese Sleep?

You may think that your Siamese should sleep in the cat bed you bought for it. Your Siamese will probably think that it should sleep in your bed—on your feet, your pillow, or your head. You, and the adults you live with, will have to decide where to allow your cat to sleep.

In general, cats prefer to sleep in warm, comfortable places. This is instinctive behavior— that is, a behavior that is not learned, but which an animal is born knowing. As hunters, sleeping in warm, cozy places helps cats to conserve energy, since they don't need to expend any energy to keep their bodies warm. That means they don't need to hunt for food as much.

A Siamese rests
in a soft bed

23

How Do You Groom a Siamese?

Most Siamese cats enjoy being brushed or combed. Brushing a cat daily keeps a cat clean. It also helps to remove loose fur, which prevents hairballs and reduces shedding.

Pet Siamese cats that do not compete in shows usually do not need to be bathed. Most cats do not enjoy being wet and do not like being bathed.

A veterinarian or other adult should trim a Siamese's nails regularly. Some people use special trimmers for this task.

Some Siamese cats develop feline acne, or chin acne, which is an infection caused by bacteria on their chin or lower lip. If your cat is prone to this, you can often prevent outbreaks by wiping its chin and face clean at least once a day with a cotton ball and warm, soapy water.

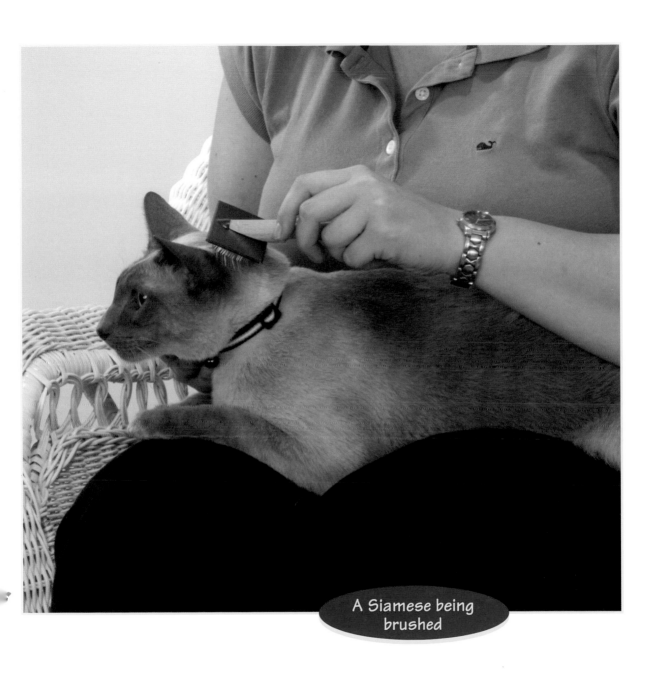

A Siamese being brushed

Can You Train Your Siamese?

Siamese cats are very smart and eager to please. Some owners enjoy teaching their cat simple tricks. For example, a Siamese might be taught to jump up into its owner's arms, take a bow, or to "sit up" on its back legs. Siamese can also learn to "fetch" and to walk on a leash. However, some people might say that Siamese cats train their owners, not the other way around.

To teach your cat not to claw your furniture, carpets, and drapes, give it a scratching post. Whenever you see your cat clawing a forbidden object, carry the cat to the scratching post. It will soon learn what you want.

You should not need to "train" your Siamese to use a litter box. Usually, while a kitten is still very young, it learns how to use a litter box by watching its mother. Then you need only to make sure that the litter box is easy to reach and keep it clean. If your cat does not use its litter box, you should consult a veterinarian on ways to train it to do so.

26

A Siamese with
a scratching post
and toy

What Kinds of Exercise or Play Are Needed?

Like all animals, Siamese cats need exercise. If your cat enjoys walking on a leash, you can make this a regular part of your routine. If not, don't worry—your cat can get plenty of exercise indoors. Any time is playtime for a Siamese.

Siamese are very intelligent and need to be kept amused. They appreciate having toys. Most Siamese love to chase balls. A lightweight plastic ball or even a wadded up piece of paper will provide lots of entertainment for your cat. Most cats also love to jump after toys that dangle from a flexible wire. Pet stores carry many products designed around this basic theme.

Cats naturally scratch at objects to pull off the worn outer layers of their claws. A scratching post gives a cat something acceptable to claw at. It also allows a cat to flex its muscles.

A Siamese kitten
plays with a ball

How Can You Help a Siamese Care for Its Young?

Taking care of the mother cat will allow her to take good care of her young. Before the kittens are born, ask your veterinarian what to feed the mother while she is pregnant (expecting young) and once she is feeding her young. Very young cats drink milk made by their mother, and this milk provides all the nutrients kittens need.

Soon after the kittens are born, you should begin getting them used to being petted and handled by humans. Your vet can advise you as to the recommended age for a kitten to be handled. Many experts recommend that kittens be handled daily. This early contact helps them bond with people, boosts their growth and development, and may improve their ability to learn.

Vets can also advise as to what age kittens should be when they have their first veterinary exam and when they should begin eating solid food.

A Siamese mother
and her young

Does a Siamese Cat Have a Point?

It sure does! In fact, it has several. "Points" are the name for the areas of darker color on a Siamese cat's coat. The darker areas in a Siamese's fur are controlled by an enzyme *(EHN zym)*—a protein that influences chemical reactions in plants and animals.

The enzyme that affects the fur of Siamese is heat-sensitive. The enzyme isn't effective at normal temperatures for a cat's body, but the enzyme becomes active in cooler areas of the cat's skin, such as the ears, legs, tail, and face. The same type of enzyme is responsible for the color camouflage of the Arctic fox. Most Arctic foxes change from brown or gray in summer to white in winter.

All Siamese kittens are pure cream-colored or white at birth because of the constant warmth inside their mother's body. Once a kitten is born, new, darker fur grows in to replace the white or cream fur. By the time a Siamese kitten is four weeks old, its points will begin to develop the color they will have when the cat is an adult.

This Siamese
kitten is just developing
its points

What Is a Purebred, Crossbred, or Pedigreed Cat?

A purebred cat is one whose mother and father belong to the same breed. A crossbred cat has parents that are both purebred cats but are of different breeds—for example, a Russian blue (see page 42) crossed with a Siamese. A pedigreed cat is a purebred that has a document or certificate showing ancestors with unmixed breeding. Most pedigrees list three to five generations of ancestors of a purebred cat.

Many people prefer the special features of a certain breed of cat. For example, such purebreds as the Siamese and the Bombay are among the most attractive and affectionate cats in the world. But cats of no specific breed may be just as beautiful and lovable as purebreds, and they are sometimes healthier.

A Bombay cat

35

What Is an
Aby Cat?

Aby is short for Abyssinian *(AB uh SIHN ee uhn)*. The word *Abyssinian* means, "having to do with Abyssinia," which is a name that was once used for the African nation of Ethiopia. People once believed the Aby cat originated in Abyssinia. Today, experts believe this cat actually originated in Asia.

The Abyssinian cat is beautiful, lean, and muscular with a long, tapering tail. This cat has a wedge-shaped head with very large ears and almond-shaped eyes.

Abys have an unusual color of coat, known as agouti *(uh GOO tee)*. Fur that is called agouti is made up of two or three bands of light and dark colors. These alternating bands of color may be red and brown, or reddish-brown and black or dark brown.

An Abyssinian

37

What Is a Colorpoint Shorthair?

A Colorpoint shorthair is a breed of short-haired cat that looks like a Siamese. It is a medium-sized cat with a slender body, blue eyes, and a colorpoint coat—that is, a body with light, solid-colored fur and contrasting points.

Colorpoint shorthairs come in red and cream, but they cannot be any unpatterned version of the four accepted colors for a Siamese—blue, chocolate, lilac, or seal (see page 12).

Colorpoints can, however, have a pattern called lynx (also sometimes called tabby) that consists of striped fur in the points; tortie, which is a patched shading of color in the points; or tortie-lynx (sometimes called tortie-tabby), which is a combination of stripes and patches in the points. This lynx, tortie, or tortie-lynx can be the usual colorpoint coloring of red or cream, but it may also be a patterned version of the usual Siamese colors.

A Colorpoint shorthair
with blue-lynx points

39

What Short-haired Cat Might Bring Luck?

At the entrance to many stores, restaurants, and even private homes in Japan you may see a small ceramic cat with one raised paw. Called a Maneki Neko (Beckoning Cat), these ceramic cats represent a breed of cat, the Japanese bobtail. This breed of cat has existed in Japan for centuries. Many Japanese consider this cat to be lucky.

This slender, medium-sized cat has a very short, rigid tail covered in bushy fur. This breed may have many colors of fur, but the traditional "good luck" color for a Japanese bobtail is white with patches of red and black.

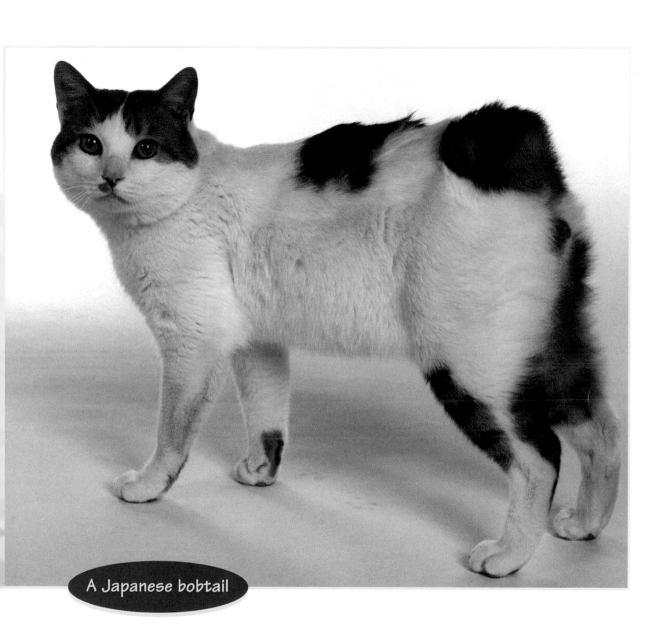

A Japanese bobtail

What Are Some Other Breeds of Short-haired Cats?

The Manx cat is named for the Isle of Man in the Irish Sea, where this breed of cat originated hundreds of years ago. Many Manx cats have an unusual feature—they have no tail!

Historians are uncertain about the origin of the Russian blue. When the breed was first shown in England in the 1870's, it was under the title "Archangel Cat." Some authorities on cats believe sailors brought this breed of cat to England from the Russian port of Archangel. The Russian blue has a short and dense coat of dark gray fur.

The Scottish fold is a medium-sized cat with ears that fold toward the face and downward. The breed was developed from a farm cat found in Scotland in 1961 that had folded ears as a result of a natural mutation (a change in hereditary material in the cell). The coat of a Scottish fold may be any color and pattern. Some varieties of Scottish folds have long fur.

A Russian blue

43

How Keen Are a Cat's Senses?

Cats have excellent hearing. They can hear frequencies much higher than humans. More than a dozen muscles control ear movement, allowing cats to rotate their ears (either together or independently) to listen for danger or prey.

Cats do not see things in sharp focus, but their eyes are much more sensitive to movement than humans' eyes are. Cats appear to be colorblind or indifferent to colors. Their eyes have a mirrorlike structure, the tapetum lucidum *(ta PEE tum LOO sih dum),* which reflects light and helps a cat to see well in dim light. This structure also produces eyeshine, the glow a person sees when light strikes the eyes of a cat at night.

Cats have a good sense of smell. It is much better than a human's, though not as good as a dog's. Cats use their sense of smell to detect enemies and to find food, mates, and their own territory, which they mark with their scent.

44

Sniffing to identify
a friend

45

How Do Cats Communicate?

Cats use sound and body language as means of communication. They meow, hiss, growl, scream, yowl, and make many other noises depending on the situation. Some experts estimate that cats can make more than 60 different sounds.

Cats may purr to communicate their emotions to people. Purring is often a sign that a cat is content, but it also can indicate an overflow of any emotion. A cat may even purr when it's furious or in pain.

Cats communicate their moods and intentions with body language. When a cat is scared, angry, or excited, its fur will stand up straight, making the cat look larger and more menacing. Its tail will fluff up like a bottle brush. In contrast, a relaxed cat with a nonfluffed tail held high is confident and happy.

The fur stands straight up on this frightened kitten

47

Why Does a Cat Twine Itself Around Your Ankles?

Your cat sometimes acts as if it is trying to trip you up. As you are walking, your cat won't stop twining itself around your ankles. At other times, as you work on your homework, your cat keeps bumping your face with its head. It seems as if your cat is just trying to tease you.

But a cat is actually doing something important as it circles your ankles or bumps you. These behaviors are called bunting. When a cat is bunting, it is marking you with a scent made in glands in its face. You can't smell it, but cats can. A cat does this to claim you as its property, or territory. Your cat is saying, "You belong to me."

Cats mark people
with their scent

49

How Can You Make Your Home Safe for a Cat?

Some things in or around your house that seem perfectly harmless can be a danger to a curious cat. Here are some tips to keep your feline friend safe:

- Keep windows closed or screened so your pet is kept safe inside.

- Keep the doors of cupboards, appliances, and closets closed to prevent your cat from getting shut inside. If you have an aquarium, make sure the hood is closed on it at all times.

- Keep electrical wires hidden—some cats may chew them.

- Never leave scraps of ribbon, string, dental floss, tinsel, or thread where a cat can reach them—cats may eat them and these items can badly harm a cat.

- Keep all medicines and chemicals out of reach.

- Don't grow plants that are toxic to cats in your house.

A Siamese views the world
from a safe perch

51

What Basic Equipment Is Needed for a Cat?

Your cat needs a litter box and litter. If you have more than one cat, you need at least one litter box for each. You will need a litter scooper.

You need food and water dishes for your cat. You may also want to get your cat a bed, though many cats prefer to sleep on a comfy chair, in a cozy corner, or on your bed.

A scratching post or scratching pad is essential. A nail trimmer and a grooming brush are also necessary items.

Your cat should have a collar (with a quick-release catch) and an I.D. tag. You will need a cat carrier for travel and veterinary visits.

Finally, a basic cat first-aid kit can be purchased at most pet stores.

A Siamese with
a cat carrier

What Is a Cat Show Like?

In most cat shows, the animals are judged on how well they conform to (match up with) the standards for that particular breed. Many different groups hold cat shows. Some shows are run by registries—groups that register particular breeds of cats.

The Cat Fanciers' Association (CFA) is the largest registry of purebred cats. This association sponsors many cat shows in the United States and some in Canada. The group has a Junior Showmanship Program designed to help young people from ages 8 through 15 to learn how to show a cat. In Junior Showmanship classes, exhibitors are not judged on the quality of the cat. Instead, the exhibitor is judged on his or her ability to handle the cat and on knowledge of the breed. This program provides young people with a great way to learn about cat shows. It also provides valuable contacts with other breeders and exhibitors who can provide advice to a beginner.

In the United Kingdom, the Governing Council of the Cat Fancy (GCCF) is a primary registry that sponsors shows.

Judging at a cat show

55

What Are Some Common Signs of Illness in Cats?

Any obvious pain or distress is a cause for concern. Also, any behavior that is not normal for your cat may be a sign that it is not feeling well. For instance, if your cat growls at you or bites at you without reason, it may be unwell. Or if your normally friendly cat hides from you, it could be ill. When in doubt, call your vet's office to discuss your concerns.

Here are some of the common signs of illness:

- Diarrhea or repeated vomiting in a cat. (All cats occasionally vomit, especially after eating grass, but repeated vomiting is not normal.)

- Wheezing sounds when breathing, or any other sign that a cat is having trouble breathing.

- A cat excessively scratching itself, especially if the scratching has caused sores.

- A cat refusing food and/or water.

56

Some scratching is
normal for a cat

What Routine Veterinary Care Is Needed?

Routine visits to the vet will help your cat to stay healthy and live a long, happy life. Cats need immunizations (shots) against viruses, including rabies and feline leukemia virus complex. They should also have a checkup at least once a year. Older cats usually have checkups more often; if your cat is 10 years or older, ask your vet about this.

Parasites can be a problem for cats. Your Siamese may develop internal parasites, such as roundworms or tapeworms. Or it may develop external ones, such as fleas or ticks. Your vet can diagnose and treat these conditions. Regular, monthly medication is often recommended to prevent heartworm infections, caused by a type of parasite.

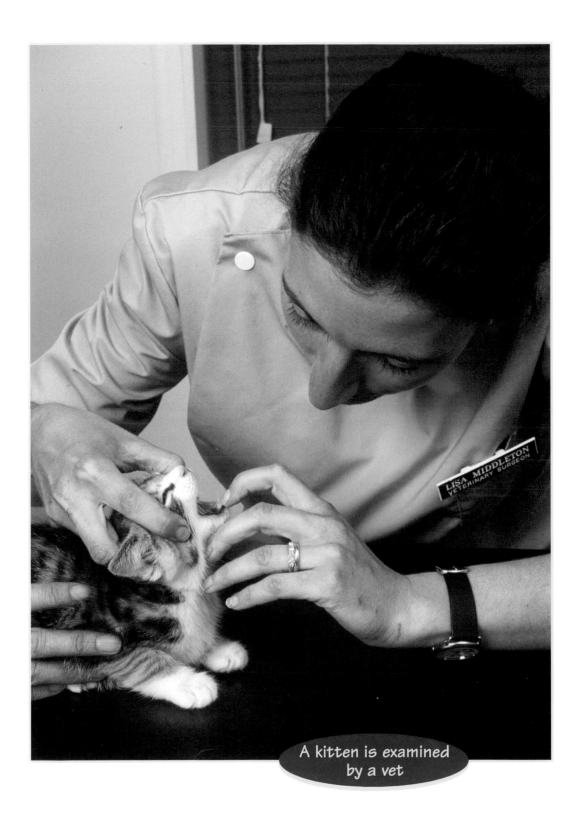

A kitten is examined
by a vet

What Are Your Responsibilities as an Owner?

As an owner, it is your responsibility to make sure your cat gets routine veterinary care. You should also watch for any signs of illness so that problems are promptly brought to the vet's attention. In addition, you should have your cat spayed or neutered.

You must feed your cat at regular times and make sure it always has fresh water. You should not leave your cat alone for long periods.

You must guard your cat's safety. If you plan to let your pet outside, make sure it is in an enclosed area from which your pet cannot escape. Your cat needs a collar and I.D. tags, as well.

Finally, think carefully before you have a cat declawed. Many humane societies feel the operation, even on just the front paws, is cruel and unnecessary, and it leaves a cat defenseless should it ever escape from its home.

Siamese watch

Short-haired Cat Fun Facts

→ The manuscript "Cat-Book Poems," written in Siam (now Thailand) sometime between 1350 and 1767, includes pictures of seal-point Siamese cats.

→ The original Siamese color was the cream-colored body with seal points.

→ All cats, even such big cats as lions, purr at about the same frequency, which is on average 25 cycles per second. Big cats, however, can only purr when they exhale. Domestic cats can purr breathing in or out.

→ A cat may spend up to 16 hours a day sleeping; older cats sleep even more.

→ The cat is the most recently domesticated mammal.

→ A group of cats is called a clowder. A litter of kittens is a kindle.

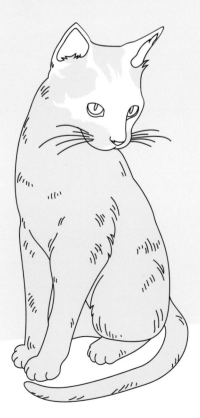

62

Glossary

breed To produce animals by carefully selecting and mating them for certain traits. Also, a group of animals having the same type of ancestors.

carnivore An animal that eats meat.

crossbred An animal produced when different breeds of an animal mate.

domestic A tame animal living with or under the care of humans. Cats, dogs, and rabbits are some domestic animals.

eyeshine The glow a person sees when light strikes the eyes of a cat at night.

feline About a cat or like a cat.

generation In animals, offspring that are at a common stage of descent from the same ancestors. For example, the young born to one set of parents at one time form one generation of cats.

gland A tissue or organ that produces and releases a useful chemical substance.

hairball A pellet or mass of hair accumulated in an animal's stomach.

hereditary Traits inherited from ancestors.

instinctive A behavior an animal is born knowing; not learned.

mammal A type of animal that feeds its young with milk made by the mother.

neuter To operate on a male animal to make it unable to produce young.

parasite An organism (living creature) that feeds on and lives on or in the body of another organism, often causing harm to the being on which it feeds.

pedigreed An animal with a document or certificate showing ancestors with unmixed breeding.

points The extremities of an animal, such as the feet, ears, and tail.

purebred An animal whose parents are known to have both belonged to one breed.

spay To operate on a female animal to make it unable to have young.

trait A feature or characteristic particular to an animal or breed of animals.

Index

(**Boldface** indicates a photo or illustration.)

acne, 24
agouti, 36, **37**
animal shelters, 18, **19**

bedding, 22, **23,** 52
body language, 46, 47
breeds, 10, 34
bunting, 48, **49**

"Cat-Book Poems," 62
cat carriers, 52, **53**
Cat Fanciers' Association, 10, 54
cats, 6; Aby (Abyssinian), 36, **37;** Archangel, 42; bodies of, 8, **9;** Bombay, 34, **35;** bunting by, 48, **49;** Burmese, 6; coats of, *see* coats; Colorpoint shorthair, 38, **39;** communication by, 46, **47;** crossbred, 34; domestic, 6, 62; essential equipment for, 52, **53;** fun facts on, 62; illness in, 54, 56, **57,** 58; Japanese bobtail, 40, **41;** lynx, 38; Manx, 6, 42; owners' responsibilities toward, 60; pedigreed, 34; purebred, 34, 54; Russian blue, 6, 34, 42, **43;** safety for, 50, **51;** Scottish fold, 42; senses of, 44, **45,** 48; short-haired, 6; Siamese, *see* Siamese cats; sleeping by, 22, **23,** 62; tabby, 38; tortie, 38; tortie-lynx,

38; veterinary care for, *see* veterinarians
cat shows, 10, **11,** 24, 54, **55**
chin acne, 24
claws, 8, 60
clowders, 62
coats: agouti, 36, **37;** colorpoint, 12, **13,** 32, 38, **39;** double, 6; single, 6

declawing, 60

enzymes, 32
eyeshine, 44

Felidae, 6
foxes, Arctic, 32
fur. *See* coats

Governing Council of the Cat Fancy, 54

hairballs, 24

Internet, 18

Junior Showmanship Program, 54

kindles, 62

kittens, **29, 33, 47,** 62; care of, 30, **31;** choosing, 16, **17**

litter boxes, 26, 52

parasites, 58
points, on coat. *See* coats
purring, 46, 62

scent, 44, **45,** 48, **49**
scratching posts, 26, **27,** 28, 52
Siamese cats, 6, **7, 51, 61;** as breed, 10, 34; beds for, 22, **23,** 52; bodies of, 8; care of young by, 30, **31;** choosing as kittens, 16, **17;** choosing older, 18, **19;** coloring of, 12, **13,** 32, 33, 62; Colorpoint shorthair compared with, 38; exercise and play for, 28, **29;** feeding, 20, **21,** 30; grooming, 24, **25;** health of, 16, 18, 24, 58; in cat shows, 10, **11,** 24, **55;** intelligence of, 26, 28; personalities of, 14, **15,** 16; sounds made by, 14; training, 26, **27;** veterinary care for, *see* veterinarians; water for, 20

tapetum lucidum, 44

veterinarians, 26, 30; care by, 24, 56, 58, **59,** 60

For more information about Siamese and Other Short-haired Cats, try these resources:

Cats, by Seymour Simon, HarperCollins Publishers, 2004

Cats: How to Choose and Care for a Cat, by Laura S. Jeffrey, Enslow Publishers, Inc., 2004

Everything Cat: What Kids Really Want to Know About Cats, by Marty Crisp, Northword Press, 2003

Smithsonian Handbooks: Cats, by David Alderton, Rebound by Sagebrush Education Resources, 2000

http://purebredcatbreedrescue.org/rescues.htm
http://www.cca-afc.com/
http://www.cfainc.org/breeds/profiles/siamese.html
http://www.gccfcats.org/

Cat Classification

Scientists classify animals by placing them into groups. The animal kingdom is a group that contains all the world's animals. Phylum, class, order, and family are smaller groups. Each phylum contains many classes. A class contains orders, an order contains families, and a family contains genuses. One or more species belong to each genus. Here is how the animals in this book fit into this system.

Animals with backbones and their relatives (Phylum Chordata)
Mammals (Class Mammalia)
Carnivores (Order Carnivora)

Cats and their relatives (Family Felidae)

  Domestic cat ....*Felis catus*